It is not about what you see,
it is about what you perceive.

Copyright © 2018 Mondå Forlag AS
3rd Edition, 2nd Print
Published by Mondå Forlag AS
ISBN: 978-82-936220-1-7

Please ask us before copying the illustrations and text in this book. We want our work to be disseminated as much as possible, so you will most probably get a positive answer from us. If you will be making money from sharing our work, or use it in a class where the teacher is paid, we may ask you for some sort of contribution. It took several years of effort to produce this book. We are nice, you will see. We might even invite you for a coffee.

We will be pleased to read your
inquiries, questions, compliments and feedback:
info@monda.no

"The Social Guidebook to Norway: An illustrated introduction"
is the first book in the series of social guidebooks to Norway. It is followed by
"The Social Guidebook to Norway 2: Friendships and Relationships"
published in June 2016.

More info: **www.thesocialguidebook.no**
Cover design and layout: Julien S. Bourrelle and Marija Hajster
Illustrations: Nicholas Lund, Ann Kristin Vangen, Elise H. Kollerud and Julien S. Bourrelle
Photograph: Jon Danielsen and Mona Hauglid
Print: Livonia Print SIA

Mondå Forlag

Mondå's vision is to make Scandinavia more connected. We believe that internationalization is not merely about creating diversity, it is about benefiting from this diversity.

The name "Mondå" is inspired by the Spanish word "el mundo" which means "the world". Mondå connects great people across cultures. It was founded in 2013 by the author of this book and quickly developed into a significant actor providing tools for companies and individuals to better understand cultural differences.

In Norway we publish books which help foreigners to socialize, work, communicate and connect with Norwegians. Norwegians learn about how their social behaviours may be perceived and how communication norms differ when working globally. We increase the competitiveness of Norwegian businesses by improving communication within multi-cultural environments.

We use humour and simple illustrations to bridge cultures.

www.monda.no

A word from the Author | Julien S. Bourrelle

This illustrated introduction to Norwegian social behaviours takes you through an eye-opening Norwegian journey. If you are Norwegian I hope it will make you smile and reflect on how special Norwegians are. If you are a foreigner, I wish you good luck meeting Norwegians and hope that this book will help you fast forward your integration.

After living and adapting to five countries, I moved to Norway. Moving to Norway has been - by far - the most challenging cultural experience of my life. In this first book, I explain the peculiar social behaviours which are first noticed when meeting Norwegians. My second book explains how Norwegians make friends and build relationships.

After five years observing and learning from Norwegians, I took a leave from my doctoral studies to write these books, lecture and to create the Mondå project.

I sincerely hope you enjoy this book. I would be happy to receive your thoughts, comments and inputs.

To Sverre, who constantly challenged his own cultural norms and allowed me to experience Norway as an insider.

Preface

The lens through which your brain sees the world shapes your reality. If you can change the lens, not only can you change the way your brain perceives other people's behaviours, but you can allow yourself to experience the world through completely different perspectives. Embedded within that statement is the key to bridging cultures and benefiting from diversity.

What you perceive or understand from what you hear and see is highly influenced by your cultural background. "Cultural intelligence" means the ability to understand the impact of individuals' cultural background on their behaviours. It is essential for effective communication and for socializing with different cultures.

Every society has its own traditions, rituals and unwritten social codes; you need to understand and learn these codes. How to greet, the distance you should keep during social interactions, the meaning of hand gestures, eye contact, and the different signs of politeness are examples of such social codes. Understanding the local social codes is a first step towards feeling at home and creating long lasting ties with people from different cultures.

We naturally feel comfortable around people who are similar to us. Abroad, we tend to connect with others from our own country, or region. We also relate more easily to people who share the same realities and experience the same challenges as we do, e.g. other foreigners from other parts of the world living in the same foreign country. Hence, international communities naturally form and isolate themselves from the host society.

When faced with different cultural norms, behaviours and traditions, we may choose to confront, complain, or conform. You can refuse to adapt your way of living, believing that your way is the right way. You may criticise your host society's beliefs and behaviours. You will find other foreigners that also confront and complain, and you will probably connect with them based on these premises; slowly isolating yourself from your host society.

The alternative path is to accept that life is different here than in your home country and start adapting your behaviours so that they do not conflict with your hosts' culture. If you are willing to experience other ways of living and communicating, and to refrain from judging local norms and values, you will grow and learn more than you could imagine. It is by far the most challenging of the three options, but also the most rewarding.

• • •

Before moving to Norway, I lived in Spain. I cannot remember anyone asking in disbelief: "Why Spain?" This is a daily question in Norway, usually followed by: "Are you planning to stay here long?" This is a paradox as Norwegians are very proud of their country and very few emigrate. They may live abroad, but most come back when the time comes to found a family: "Ja, vi elsker dette landet". Yes, Norwegians love their country; and for good reasons.

Norway is in its golden age, at least economically. With the discovery of oil in the North Sea and the sustainable management of its economic resources, Norway ranks as one of the fastest growing economies of the western world with one of the world's highest Human Development Index (HDI) and GDP per capita. Norway is a safe place to live where people are trusting, trustworthy and well educated. Most police officers do not carry firearms (still), and many Norwegians do not lock their doors; they do not need to. The standard of living is very high, with single-family housing accessible to the middle class and spacious natural environments. Most Norwegian families own a second residence. Higher education is free and students enjoy the world's best levels of governmental financial support.

The cities are small, clean, well-organised and unpolluted. People come from all around the world to admire Norway's stunning fjords and mountains, and its pristine nature. Norwegians themselves are quite beautiful, and that keeps many of us here! The welfare system is one of the world's most generous and provides the very best family support. Everyone is considered equal and few social classes exist. There is a strong feeling of community where everyone is expected and willing to contribute to society. People respect each other; it is a peaceful place where people are not aggressive and where criminality rates are low.

This sounds like the perfect place to live. Why then are Norwegians surprised that foreigners would choose to live in this great country at the top of the world?

Two things make it challenging; the climate and connecting with Norwegians. I could also add the food. Norwegians are peaceful, helpful and trustworthy. They are often shy, reserved, well behaved, well organised, calm, efficient, pragmatic and serious. When Norwegians are sober, rigid norms frame their social interactions. If you do not obey these unwritten social norms, you may easily end up not succeeding socially. This changes with alcohol and the contrast can be shocking.

Understanding the peculiar Norwegian social dynamics, behaviours and norms is difficult and it takes time and effort. You need to take initiatives, but carefully and within a well-defined social framework. You need to understand why, how and where social interactions take place.

A lot has been written on what it means to be "typisk norsk". This guidebook differentiates between typical Norwegian behaviours and behaviours that are peculiar to Norwegians. By being aware of these peculiar behaviours, we can bridge the cultural gap at home in Norway, but also when doing business abroad. This guidebook will make your experience in Norway even more enriching and valuable by teaching you how to connect with Norwegians and enjoy not only the country, but also its people and their splendid society.

*Do not trust what you perceive;
strive to understand what is meant.*

Julien S. Bourrelle
julien@monda.no

This book is full of generalisations and stereotypes.
It draws an image of Norwegians that can be criticized.
I encourage you to do so.
Use the press and social media.

The International Bubble

Social interactions are easier between people that resemble each other
That share the same realities
The same challenges

Social bubbles naturally form around foreign communities

Understand why and you will understand how to prevent it
It often takes a conscious effort to get out of such a social bubble

You need to learn the unwritten social codes of your new society
To actively participate in activities that are common for locals
Experience a new way of life
New food
New rituals
New traditions
New perspectives
New values
New languages

You need to limit the amount of time you spend with fellow foreigners
Be more conscious about your own biases
Your expectations
Your perceptions

Locals who want to connect with foreigners need to do the exact same thing
To be open to different ways of life

Frame Activity and Social Bubbles

In Norway, the international bubble is one of many bubbles

Norwegians are special people
They socialize around "frame activities"
Sports, games, organisations, etc.
They form social bubbles
They take part in many bubbles, but the bubbles do not interact
They are rigid
They do not mix

Outsiders may not be invited to join activities organised within a bubble
Even if the activity does not relate to the bubble's "frame activity"

For example, a sports group going to have a beer
It would be challenging to invite someone who is not part of the team to join for the beer
It is not about you being a foreigner or that they do not like you
It is because you are not part of the right frame

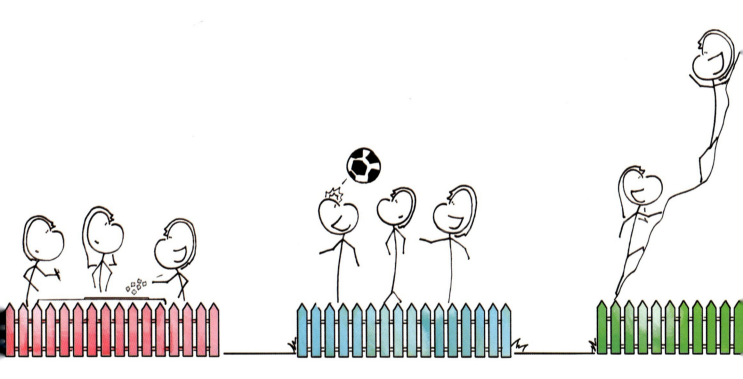
The Social Guidebook to Norway

Bubble Hopping

Get involved
Really
Get involved
Join frame activities
Many frames
Fill up your schedule with bubbles
Hop from one social bubble to another

You will feel Norwegian
And be socially active like a Norwegian

The Social Guidebook to Norway

Activities with a Purpose

Norwegians like to do things by themselves
They may send you letters to ask you to clean the street and the park nearby
Or paint the apartment block
Or at work to assemble new furniture and change the decoration
Do it
It is called dugnad

Interactions are pragmatic at first
You are only allowed purposeful communication related to the activity
Interactions become warmer after the purposeful work is done
Manual work provides a frame for socialization
You may even be invited for dinner after the manual work

The Social Guidebook to Norway

Attempting to socialize without a frame can be challenging
Norwegians may be suspicious of your intentions
They may try to figure out why you are talking to them
What you are after

The Social Guidebook to Norway

The Need for a Frame

With an acquaintance
You will go to a quiz rather than for a coffee
You will play a game rather than discussing the news
You will go walking in the mountains rather than reflecting together on the world

If you want to discuss politics, sign up in a political organisation
If you want to discuss art, sign up in an art club
If you want to discuss feelings, get an appointment with a psychologist

Norwegians socialize best doing something practical rather than simply talking

A typical conversation in many places around the world could look something like this

A simple comment opens the door to an interesting answer
The conversation flows easily

The Social Guidebook to Norway

Norwegian Conversations

In Norway it may not flow as easily

Conversations are direct
Simple
Pragmatic

Unframed discussions are not a usual means to getting to know people

Social Logic

In many countries around the world, you may naturally greet strangers
And start talking
For no particular reason

You end up talking for a little while

Purposeful activities follow from interesting conversations
And a curiosity for getting to know new people
This is the typical timeline

A

B

C

The Social Guidebook to Norway

In Norway, things work a bit differently

First, you sign up in a "blåbærplukkerforening" (Organisation for the Picking of Blueberries)
You meet up in the forest and you work purposefully for several hours - mostly in silence
Purposeful communication may take place around practical aspects of picking berries
Because it is practical, you walk down the mountain together
And because you both are hungry, and have food in your hands, you have a reason to eat together

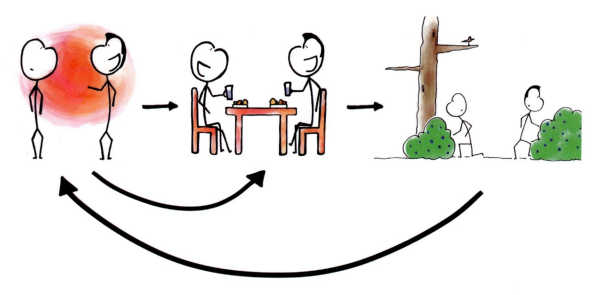

In Norway, dinners are not a means of getting to know people
They are a result of an established relationship

This is key to understanding the Norwegian socialization logic
Do not invite a Norwegian you just met to share a meal
You may never see him again

Get involved
Take part in organised and purposeful activities

The Social Guidebook to Norway

Greetings

In Spain
Like many other places around the world
You greet people
When arriving at work
When leaving an event
When entering a shop

People turn around and greet you back
Often with a smile

The Social Guidebook to Norway

In Norway, it works a little bit differently

The Social Guidebook to Norway

The meaning of Norwegian Greetings

You greet when there is a practical reason to do so
If you have something to discuss
If you want to start a conversation
If you need help

If your colleagues leave without saying goodbye in the afternoon
They do not intend to be rude
They are in fact very polite
Norwegian polite

They do not want to disturb

Keep in mind that social norms are different in Norway

In some cultures, people greet each other every morning at work
For no obvious reason

They go around shaking hands and kissing each other
Including those they haven't met before
It takes half an hour

If they are in a hurry and cannot greet properly
They will try to establish eye contact
And nod

They do the same when entering and leaving conferences and parties
It is part of their ritual
Of their social norms
Part of being polite in their culture

The Social Guidebook to Norway

Do not be surprised if your Norwegian neighbour passes just in front of you
Without looking at you
Without greeting you
As if you did not exist
As if you were invisible

He is not rude, nor impolite
He is actually very polite
He does not want to disturb

He will talk to you if there is a practical reason to do so
If something is wrong with the garden
If he is unpleased by something

If your neighbours, colleagues and acquaintances do not greet you and small talk
It does not mean they do not like you
They are just trying to be polite
Norwegian polite

If you meet in another setting where there is a reason to speak
Like in «syden» or at «bymarka»
It will provide a comfortable framework and a practical reason to speak to you

The Social Guidebook to Norway

Politeness

In Norway, politeness is much more about not disturbing others
Social codes, norms and manners are different

Respecting privacy, space and silence is often more important
You do not disturb someone only to greet them without a purpose
You avoid speaking loudly in public places to respect others
You avoid looking at someone for no reason
You leave space
Both physically and psychologically

Norwegians are practical, purposeful and efficient in their politeness

And since Norwegians are polite
And want to prevent confrontations
They won't disturb you to tell you if you are being impolite in their eyes

The Social Guidebook to Norway

Introductions

When you meet someone you know
You introduce the person you are with
This is basic politeness
In most places

Meeting a Norwegian Friend

In Norway, it works differently
You will be introduced if there is a practical reason to do so

Otherwise, you may be left standing not knowing what to do
It is not meant as a rude, impolite or uneducated behaviour
It is simply more efficient and less risky not to introduce you
It prevents a potentially awkward conversation
Between people part of different social bubbles

Feeling Comfortable

Norwegians need two things in order to feel comfortable communicating with others
A reason to speak
And an opportunity to escape

When Norwegians have the possibility to escape
They feel safe
They greet
They small talk
For no reason

There is an organisation to frame all of this
It is called "Den Norske Turistforening"

The opposite of this is one of the most awkward places I have experienced
A Norwegian elevator

You feel a heavy atmosphere
Do not greet
Do not talk
Do not look at the other people
Do not smile
It will just make things worse

In an elevator you are missing both the frame and the opportunity to escape
It is a very uncomfortable place for Norwegians

The Social Guidebook to Norway

The Norwegian Dream

Lose yourself in the mountains away from everyone
And from everything
No road
No water
No electricity
They call it "Hytte"

I thought it was to save money
It is not

Norwegians will spend a large part of their savings
To buy such a place
To be alone
In the middle of nowhere

They prefer spending their money on being alone and living simply
Rather than flying to the south of Europe every vacations
And stay in five star hotels

They will buy a hytte where they need to
Carry their food on their shoulders for kilometers
Get water with buckets from a stream
Light the place with candles
Go to the toilet outside

The Social Guidebook to Norway

Norwegians will also use their savings to help «Africa» because they feel people there
Carry their food on their shoulders for kilometers
Get water with buckets from a stream
Light the place with candles
Go to the toilet outside

The Social Guidebook to Norway

The most remote island in the world is called Bouvet Island
It belongs to Norway
Long story
What did the Norwegian government do when they got the island?

They built a hytte!
It is the most isolated hytte in the world
And probably the most valuable hytte in the world

Being Alone

Norwegians find ways of being alone in cities as well
They value their personal space as much as their opportunities to be alone

They will travel alone to work
Rather than organising to commute with colleagues
It is much more efficient and practical
And you do not need to talk to anyone

The Social Guidebook to Norway

They also eat alone
You do not need to talk
It is a practical and efficient way to feed oneself quickly
You can then go home early
Or go training
Alone

The Social Guidebook to Norway

Personal Space

This is when you know that a Norwegian bus stop is full
And that you need to stand

The Social Guidebook to Norway

Actually this is just part of the picture

Norwegians love their personal space
Make sure to leave space when standing as well

The Social Guidebook to Norway

At conferences, a foreigner may start to talk with a Norwegian
The foreigner will talk at a distance that feels comfortable to him
The Norwegian, feeling invaded in his personal space, will take a small step back
The foreigner, being interested to get to know the Norwegian, will step closer
Reestablishing a comfortable distance for himself

This distance is not comfortable for the Norwegian
The Norwegian steps back again
And a little dance begins

Keep your distance and Norwegians will feel comfortable

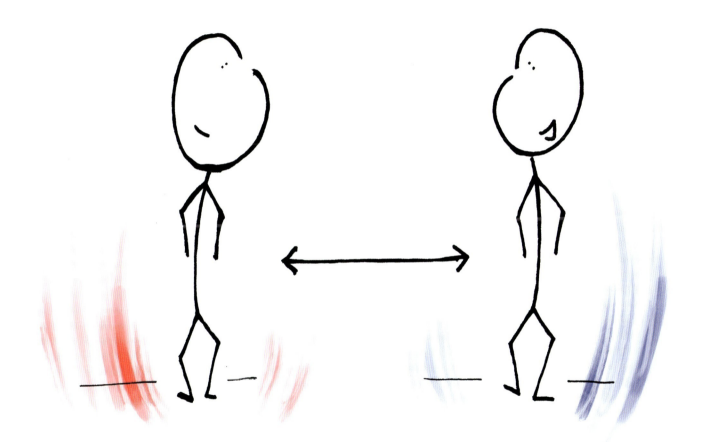

The Social Guidebook to Norway

The Norwegian Nature

Norwegians proudly go outdoors in difficult weather conditions
They do not talk
The wind and rain makes it impossible
It gives Norwegians a great feeling
A feeling of accomplishment

Norwegians' relationship to nature is unique
« Det finnes ikke dårlig vær
Bare dårlige klær »*

Kids are raised that way
They are forced to go outside in harsh conditions from a young age

When they have done it enough times
They also start to believe that this is enjoyable

* There is no such thing as bad weather, only bad clothing

The Social Guidebook to Norway

Suffering and Pain

Norwegians enjoy physical pain
Or at least it seems like they do
Jumping into cold fjords
Rolling in the snow naked
Walking hours in freezing rain and wind
Jogging on icy roads in the winter darkness

Pain does not really exist anyway
This is not sufferance
It is enjoyment

And the «hytte» seems so much more enjoyable afterwards
And it provides a boost to your social status on Monday morning at work

The Social Guidebook to Norway

Birken is a 54 km ski race over mountains and valleys
Thousands of Norwegian businessmen participate every year
It is one of the few arenas where they are allowed to boost their social status

Do well and the largest national business newspaper will publish your name and race time
Together with the name of the company you work for and your position there
By showing publicly that you have great physical abilities,
That you are in good shape
That you endure pain under the cold for several hours in silence
You will increase your credibility, trust and respect
In the eyes of your Norwegian bosses, employees and clients

If you are good at skiing
Mention it in job interviews
Even the royals take part in this competition

This is beautiful
Where else in the world would it be safe enough for a future King to ski in public for 54 km?

Cross-Country Skiing

Sport often practiced alone in the dark under freezing temperatures
And requiring no communication

A very Norwegian sport

The Social Guidebook to Norway

Gender Interaction

Ever since I was 12 years old, I have been told
To open doors for women
To walk on the right side of the sidewalk
To serve wine to women first

When I got to Norway, women told me they could open doors themselves
That I should not change side to walk between them and the cars
And they were suspicious that I was trying to get them drunk when serving them wine

Norwegian Women

Norwegian women are independent
Very independent
Gender-based politeness norms have mostly disappeared
And it is often considered as a good thing

A Norwegian woman without a man
is like a fish without a bicycle

Welcome to Norway
Where genders may relate differently

The Social Guidebook to Norway

Complimenting

Men around the world compliment women
It is part of the social ritual in many countries
Women usually appreciate and expect compliments

Norwegian men tend to be more practical

They will imply compliments
Rather than voicing them directly

For good reasons
They learnt that paying too much attention
And giving direct compliments to Norwegian women
May not get the desired results

Norwegian women love to be independent and free

Norwegian women are not used to receiving compliments
Keep that in mind
They may appreciate it
Or not
Do not overdo it
You may easily scare a Norwegian
While French and Italians are experts in the art of seduction

The Social Guidebook to Norway

Norwegian men are a little more practical

They have learnt that if they do like the French or the Italian
They may never see the Norwegian woman again

They express the same thing
But they do it in a more subtle manner

"Not only did I notice you had eyes, but I noticed they were blue"

They indicate to a woman that they noticed her
Which is already a big thing in Norway

Be sincere in your praise and subtle in your compliments

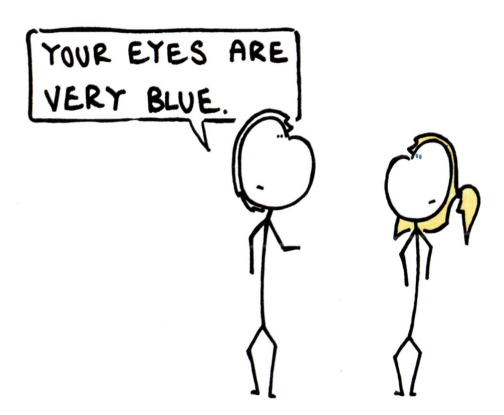

GENDER EQUALITY

The Norwegian culture idealises the idea that both genders have the same roles in society

Kids grow up with the idea that no difference exists between boys and girls
There is no such thing as gender roles in Norway

The result is an equal society

To a foreign eye
Men's behaviours may appear feminine
Women's behaviours may appear masculine
Both care for children
Lead businesses
Do manual work
Work as police officers and soldiers

The following situation is considered totally normal in Norway

The Social Guidebook to Norway

And so is this one
Men and women have interchangeable roles in the Norwegian society

The Social Guidebook to Norway

While Norway ranks high on gender equality
Genders interact little
They are part of different bubbles

Genders interact when necessary
When there is a reason to do so
When it is practical and purposeful

Do not be surprised to see women and men in separate groups
At work, in conferences, at parties

Norwegian Party Timeline

Kl 19.00

Kl 22.55

The Social Guidebook to Norway

They will mix if there is a reason to
This is a bit like the social bubbles we discussed earlier

Alcohol helping
Things becomes easier

Kl 23.00
It is time to go to town now.

The Social Guidebook to Norway

The Norwegian Dating Model

Dating in Norway requires some adaptation
After experimenting for some time
I started to appreciate the Norwegian way

In most countries around the world,
When you meet a woman you like
You say "hi"

HEI!

The Social Guidebook to Norway

And you invite her for a date

If that works well ...

You invite her for a second date

If that works well ...

The Social Guidebook to Norway

You invite her for a dinner

... and if that works well ...

Then maybe something else happens!

The Social Guidebook to Norway

This is the normal timeline
In most countries around the world

In Norway
It works a little bit differently

Then there is a fast forward process

If you wake up the next morning and the person is still next to you
You invite for a date

You go back here

If that still works well
And only then
Can you say hi if you meet in the hallway

Then you invite for a second date
And then for dinner

Because dinners in Norway are a result of an established relationship,
not a way of getting to know people!

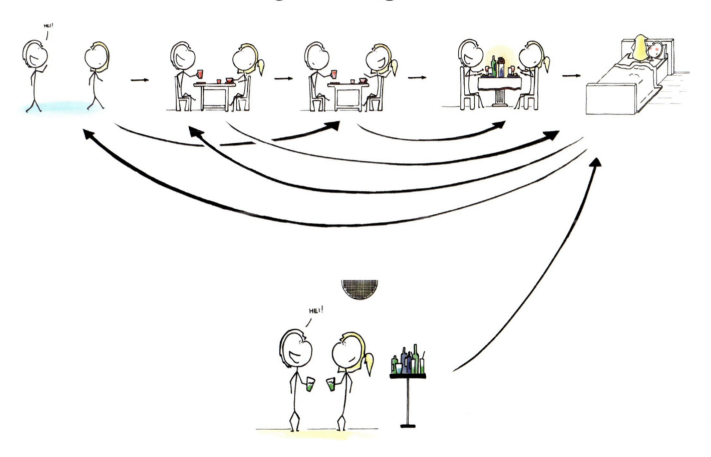

There are several reasons for these traditions
One is the difficulty to ask people on a date

Everything comes into place here
The frames
The fear of awkward conversations
The small talk
The need for space

As a man, you learn to be very careful when inviting a woman outside a frame activity

The Social Guidebook to Norway

Alcohol helping
Things become easier

A lot of things become easier with alcohol
Everyone says "hi" and small talk
People stand close to each other
Men give each other hugs and a lot of physical contact
They compensate for the difficult sober state
And the contrast can be surprising at times

The Social Guidebook to Norway

Norwegians become curious
And happy to talk with strangers
They become much more expressive
And take social initiatives
Alcohol helping
You make new friends easily

The Social Guidebook to Norway

However
What happens during the weekends
Stays there

Norwegians have many frame activities during the week
It keeps them busy
They may not have time to chat
To hang out

They may not be able to invite you to join their frame activities either
You need to be part of the group first
You need to register in the organisation

It is not that Norwegians do not care about you
You just need to join groups as well

The relationship Norwegians enjoy with alcohol can be surprising
A few days after I first came to Norway
I wanted to explore the city at night
I saw beautiful blond Norwegian women
In nice dresses
And men in ties
Crawling on the sidewalks

They call it "fadderuke"
Fadderuke is the first two weeks in the beginning of the university studies
Norwegians are given alcohol, locked into groups and forced to socialize around activities
This is where Norwegians find their friends for life

The Social Guidebook to Norway

Emotions

The way Norwegians express feelings is subtle
Refrain from showing negative feelings
Anger, frustration or any type of aggression
Positive feelings you may express, but keep it subtle

Be excited without moving your body
Be happy in silence
Except when watching cross-country skiing
Or drinking

Unless you come from Finland
Norwegian emotional feedback will be challenging to interpret

Feedback

If your colleagues have feedback
Positive or negative
They may wait for a specific day of the year to tell you

This is feedback day
They call it "julebord"
Julebord is the grown up version of fadderuke

It is a good idea to explain to foreigners what a julebord is
I was slightly surprised the first time it happened to me

The Social Guidebook to Norway

The Norwegian Egalitarian Society

In Norway, we try not to make anyone feel better or worse than others
We make people feel good
Good enough
Good enough is enough

If you are "too" good
You will feel pressure to be just good enough

You will not get special attention
You will not be praised in special ways
Those who haven't performed as good as you did
Won't feel bad about themselves

If you are struggling
The society will help you to be good enough
You will be praised for your effort
And what you manage to accomplish

Norwegians may rather praise those who haven't delivered the best results
But which made an effort to produce below expectation results
Norwegians do not want to make those who lag behind feel less worthy

This is at the core of the Norwegian education system
Of the labour laws
And a corner stone of how we interact with people at work

That's amazing!
Great job!

This was bad.
You better do much better next time.

We encourage, we help others
And in the end, no one should believe that they are better than others
Foreigners may find it challenging
Especially if used to a competitive society that pushes you to be best

At work and in relationships in Norway
You may be unsure
If people like you or not
If your work is appreciated or not
If people are happy or not

Feedback is subtle in Norway
Learn to interpret feedback
In terms of what it means in the cultures of those who give it to you
This is all about perceptions
If you do not receive suggestions on how to do better
It usually means that it is ok
Not exceptional nor bad
It is good enough

Janteloven
(The unofficial Scandinavian Social Law)

1. You're not to think you are anything special.
2. You're not to think you are as good as we are.
3. You're not to think you are smarter than we are.
4. You're not to convince yourself that you are better than we are.
5. You're not to think you know more than we do.
6. You're not to think you are more important than we are.
7. You're not to think you are good at anything.
8. You're not to laugh at us.
9. You're not to think anyone cares about you.
10. You're not to think you can teach us anything.

NOTE: Janteloven is not directed towards foreigners, but towards Scandinavians themselves.

Refrain from showing success or achievements
Never brag
Except in sports
Be humble
If you do well and pretend to be average
The society will praise you for this

If kids excel at school
They will not be pushed further or put into special classes or schools
They will be encouraged to help those who struggle

Kids learn to assist each other
The most clever kids learn to take care of those who struggle
Helping the weak lies at the basis of the Norwegian social democratic model
Actually the whole welfare system of the Nordics is based on these premises

The Social Guidebook to Norway

In other countries, kids are often not encouraged to help others
They should rather focus on their own work
Strive to become best at what they do
And obey strict discipline imposed by an authority figure

If they do good
They will be moved to a special class
And then a special school
Additional resources will be invested
So they can develop to their full potential
So that they become excellent rather than merely good enough

Showing social status is very important in some places around the world
Teachers will assert their higher status over students
From kindergarten to university
They will refer to themselves with special titles
They will ask students to address them in a special polite form
They will dress in ways that assert their higher status
Business executives will do the same

After all, everyone had the same opportunity to succeed
And since they focused on their own work and did better than others
It appears acceptable that they show their higher value

In Norway, equality is understood differently

IN NORWAY,
EQUALITY IS NOT ABOUT EQUALITY OF OPPORTUNITY
IT IS ABOUT EQUALITY OF RESULTS

Norwegian Equality

The wellbeing of society prevails over providing individuals with equal opportunities

There is a shared understanding that the «strong» shall help the «weak»
so that all stand equal in the end

Or that

The most talented help the less gifted so that all end up being average

Equality can be understood as providing equal support to everyone

It can also be understood as providing those who struggle with extra resources
so that they have an equal chance of success as those who already are good
This is the Norwegian approach

In other places around the world
Everyone has the same opportunity to get extra resources if they perform well
In such a system you will put requirements on these extra resources
Only the best will be good enough to fulfil the requirements and get the extra support
They will then have an opportunity to become excellent
To develop to their full potential
This is how scholarships work in many countries

In Norway the government gives scholarship to anyone who wish to study
They call it Lånekasse
The Loan Box
Everyone get the same scholarship if they want to study
Independently of their potential
Or the relevance of their studies

The Social Guidebook to Norway

In Norway
Equality of results aims to ensure a balance in different groups of society
With all the benefits that this diversity entails

The means put forward to reach that equality can appear unequal

Norwegians use quotas to ensure equality of results
Gender points are given to enter programmes at university
Leadership training is offered, often only for one gender

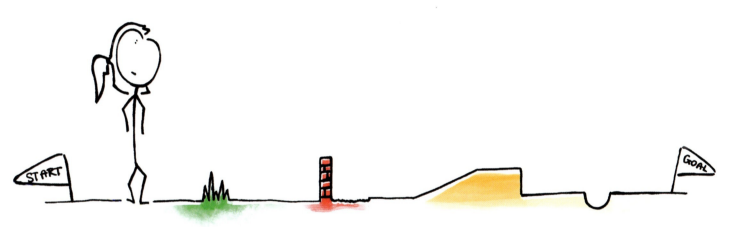

The Social Guidebook to Norway

Not Equality of Opportunity

From an outsider's perspective
It may feel like you are being discriminated
It may feel unfair
It may feel contradictory to what equality stands for

You may be denied education
You may be denied access to certain networks
You may not be able to get funding easily
Because you are of a particular gender

The Social Guidebook to Norway

Equality of Results

The wellbeing of society prevails over providing equal treatment to everyone

Do not worry
It is positive discrimination

Not everyone in Norway believes that discrimination can be positive
The constitution is pretty clear on this
Especially when it comes to education - §109

The good side of the Norwegian Egalitarian Society

There is a good balance in society
With little social classes
Little crime

Even if it may sometimes feel unfair on an individual basis

From the production line to the top management
Everyone can talk to each other
Problem can be solved quickly
It provides Norway with a competitive advantage
And makes it a very enjoyable place to live

The Social Guidebook to Norway

Norway is a great country

After all
Det er typisk norsk å være god*

Janteloven only applies for individuals
Not for Norway as a society
Norway is best

Especially in cross country skiing
Norway is best in the world
Norwegians are very proud of that
Proud of being best in the world
At a sport practiced by a handful of Northern countries

*«It is typically Norwegian to be good» is a well-known quote from the then Norwegian Prime Minister, Gro Harlem Brundtland (1992)

Trust and Honesty

Equality of results and few social class differences bring positive aspects
People communicate better
Everyone has enough income
Norwegians are honest and trustful

Do not worry if you leave your laptop unattended in a coffee shop
Or if you forget your mobile phone on the bus
Nicholas, our illustrator, does this every month
He always gets it back

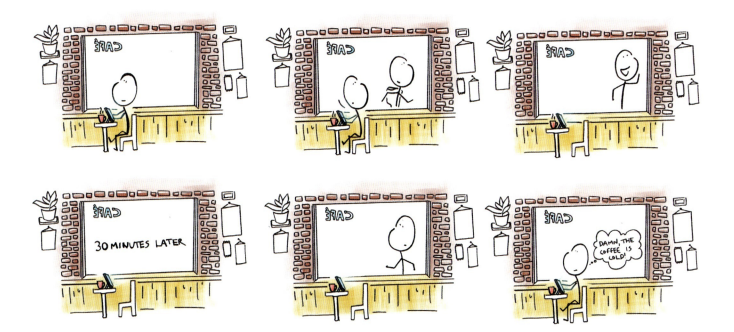

The Social Guidebook to Norway

You can trust that Norwegians
Will show up on time
Will deliver what they said they would deliver
At the time they said they would deliver it
And at the quality level they said they would deliver it

You can trust that what Norwegians claim they can do is true
They will not brag about themselves
About their achievements
About who they know
About how much money they make

They are humble, honest and trustful people

They are well organised
And precise when it comes to time
They work short hours
But are very effective
Both at work and at home
Combining a life where both parents work
Requires a strict schedule

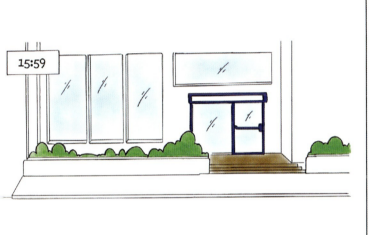

The Social Guidebook to Norway

Even if Norwegians may appear special
They are very nice people
Just a little peculiar sometimes

It makes it easy to recognise them abroad
When you see this man in a foreign airport
You can go straight to him and say
«Hei, hva heter du?»

The Social Guidebook to Norway

Social status is expressed differently in Norway
While in most places a man in a suit would link him to the highest social classes
A man carrying things on his shoulders would belong to the lowest social classes
For Norwegian men, it is just practical to have a backpack

Just like running shoes for a Norwegian woman
Norwegian women are pragmatic
They want to wear shoes that allow them
To easily jump over a stream
Cross a snowfield
Or climb a mountain

While a woman in a dress wearing running shoes
Is common sight in Norway
It may be slightly unexpected in other places around the world

In many places women are judged by the elegance of their shoes
Some people abroad may have difficulties to know how to relate to running shoes

The Social Guidebook to Norway

If you forget what I wrote in this book
Think about a wild cat
You need to be slow, careful, playful, and distant
You also need to take initiatives
Play games for a few hours, a few days, or a few years
And you will make Norwegian friends
Once you are friends, you are friends for life

However, friendships mean something different in Norway
Just like relationships

The second book in this series of social guidebooks to Norway deals with friendships and relationships

Norwegians are great people
You just need to learn to connect in the way they are used to
This first book provided some tips
Get involved
Take initiative
Leave space

ENJOY NORWAY!

The Social Guidebook to Norway

ACKNOWLEDGEMENTS

Elise Halvorsen Kollerud – For your constant support, availability and hard work

Nicholas Lund – For your constant creativity and energy

Sverre Haug Lindseth – For your clever reflections

Pellegrino Riccardi – For inspiring, for your inputs, for your support

Maman – For the unconditional support and constant encouragement

Erik Villum – For believing in me and the potential of this project

Marius Svenungsen – For for your logic, organisation and discipline

Carl Johan and Siv – For your shared passion in connecting people

Anders and Lennart – For facilitating the first edition of this book through Frisk Forlag

Javed M. Saeed – For the help through Millor

Kathleen Mathisen – For having taken early step which allowed this project to flourish

Pierre Puggaard – For opening the doors of Frogner House and our great collaboration

Bård Wallentinsen – For your useful feedback and help

Katy Paus – For your enthusiasm and very useful review

And for your useful inputs in both books: **Birgit Skarstein, Thomas Bergflødt, Jon Mikkel Haugen, Hans Myraune, Maria Amelie, Lisa Cooper, Kristine Sommerseth Bjartness, Amalie Holt and Andy Carter.**

Thank you for allowing me to connect with great people
And make this project so successful

SIKT

Sprudlevann

Ett bord

Alarga

Start

Frisk Forlag

Frogner House Apartment in Oslo

Millor

Nova

Subaru

Read more about our collaborators: www.thesocialguidebook.no/collaborators

Thank you as well to all the nice people working at ARK, Norli and Tanum which made it possible to reach out to the whole of Norway with our social guidebooks.

About the Author

Julien S. Bourrelle

MSc. Rocket Science

Made in Canada

Lived in Australia, Canada, Germany, New Zealand, Spain, Norway

Speaks French, English, Spanish, Norwegian

Email: julien@monda.no
Twitter: @_juliens
Instagram: juliensbourrelle
Snapchat: juliensb

Photographers:
Jon Danielsen / Mona Hauglid (TEDxArendal)

> "I believe that integration starts with mutual understanding, and that foreigners should be provided with adequate tools to understand their host society."

As Steve Jobs said: "You can never connect the dots looking forward, you can only connect the dots looking backwards". At twenty years old, I could only speak French and I had never been outside Canada. Ten years later, I could speak four languages fluently and I had lived in five countries.

I studied mechanical engineering at McGill University in Montréal, with stays at the University of Western Australia and at the University of Auckland. I specialised in astrodynamics, a sub-field of rocket science at the Technical University of Munich and the Polytechnic University of Madrid under a scholarship from the European Commission.

I then moved to a little town in the middle of Norway, to the beautiful city of Trondheim, to take a doctoral degree at the Norwegian University of Science and Technology (NTNU). Each time I moved to a different country, I made a conscious effort to adapt my behaviours to the local norms, to learn the language, to integrate. My adaptation to Norway has been the most challenging cultural experience of my life. When I finally cracked the Norwegian code, I started to help others understand these peculiar Norwegians.

I became the first foreigner to sit on the board of directors of the Norwegian Universuty of Scinece and Technology since the foundation of the university in 1910, I led the doctoral organisation and I sat on the Norwegian National Research committee (UHR). In 2013, I took a leave from my studies in order to hold lectures about the Norwegian culture. I founded Mondå Forlag the year after, a publishing house with a vision to bridge culture by providing entertaining yet useful tools to help connect great people. We help Norwegian businesses to better benefit from diversity.

This is the 3rd edition of *The Social Guidebook to Norway* our flagship book first published in 2014. Thanks to a visit to NRK Lindmo Norway's biggest Saturday night show many Norwegians learnt about our work. Soon afterwards I received the Top 10 award from HRH Crown Prince Haakon which highlight an «outstanding international role model in the Norwegian working and social life». It provided me with great motivation to continue develop tools that bridge culture. The way forward includes new books, collaborations with authors and entrepreneurs passionate about culture and the idea of benefitting from diversity. I hope you enjoyed this first book and that you will read the other ones in the series.

Julien S. Bourrelle

"We all would benefit better from diversity if locals and foreigners were provided with adequate tools to understand each other's biases, expectations and perceptions."

Also in "The Social Guidebook to Norway" series

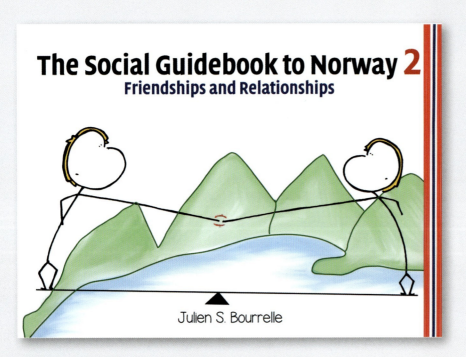

"Friendships and Relationships" continues the Norwegian adventure started in this book. It presents 100 new illustrations taking you through the funny peculiarities of Norwegian relationships.

www.thesocialguidebook.no/2

Also published by Mondå Forlag

This book presents 100 unwritten social laws that Norwegians follow, but will most probably never tell you!

It is an adaptation to English of
Egil Aslak A. Hagerup's bestseller **Norges uskrevne lover.**
It will make you laugh, smile and give you valuable insights into the Norwegian social dynamic.

www.unwrittenlaws.no/100laws

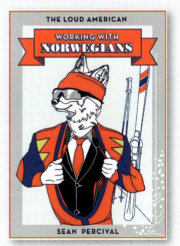

For non-Norwegians: This is the greatest book EVER written about working with Norwegians. It's better than all other books on the Norwegian culture. It will make you smarter, better looking and more successful. You must have this book. Buy it now!

For Norwegians: This book is about working with Norwegians. It is not any better than other books, but some people believe it is good. Not excellent, but good enough. It tells you how you may be perceived at work. You can buy it if you want, but you do not need to.

www.workingwithnorwegians.no/la

All books by Mondå Forlag

ISBN 978-82-936220-1-7 The Social Guidebook to Norway: An illustrated introduction
ISBN 978-82-690072-3-7 The Social Guidebook to Norway 2: Friendships and Relationships
ISBN 978-82-93622-10-9 The Social Guidebook to Norway (Chinese translation)
ISBN 978-82-93622-00-0 The 100 Unwritten Norwegian Social Laws
ISBN 978-82-690072-9-9 The Loud American: Working with Norwegians

ISBN 978-82-690072-1-3 Nordmenn: En illustrert innføring
ISBN 978-82-690072-7-5 Nordmenn 2: Vennskap og kjærlighet

ISBN 978-82-93622-08-6 The Swedes: A happy culture of Scandinavia
ISBN 978-82-93622-09-3 Working with Swedes

Order online with discount code "MondaBooks"

Illustrating cultures
www.monda.no

Online Norwegian cultural resources

TEDx Talk by Julien S. Bourrelle «Learn a New Culture»
«How Culture Shapes Behaviours»

Mondå illustrated blog www.thesocialguidebook.no

Facebook page «I Fucking Love Norway»
«The Social Guidebook to Norway»

Mondå Forlag website www.monda.no

Sign up for newsletter on **www.thesocialguidebook.no**
to receive further resources and updates on our new books.

It is not about diversity,
It is about benefiting from diversity.

Your personal observations about Norwegians:

The Social Guidebook to Norway